THE CARDIO

THE CARDIO - SUJITHA SURESH

SUJITHA SURESH

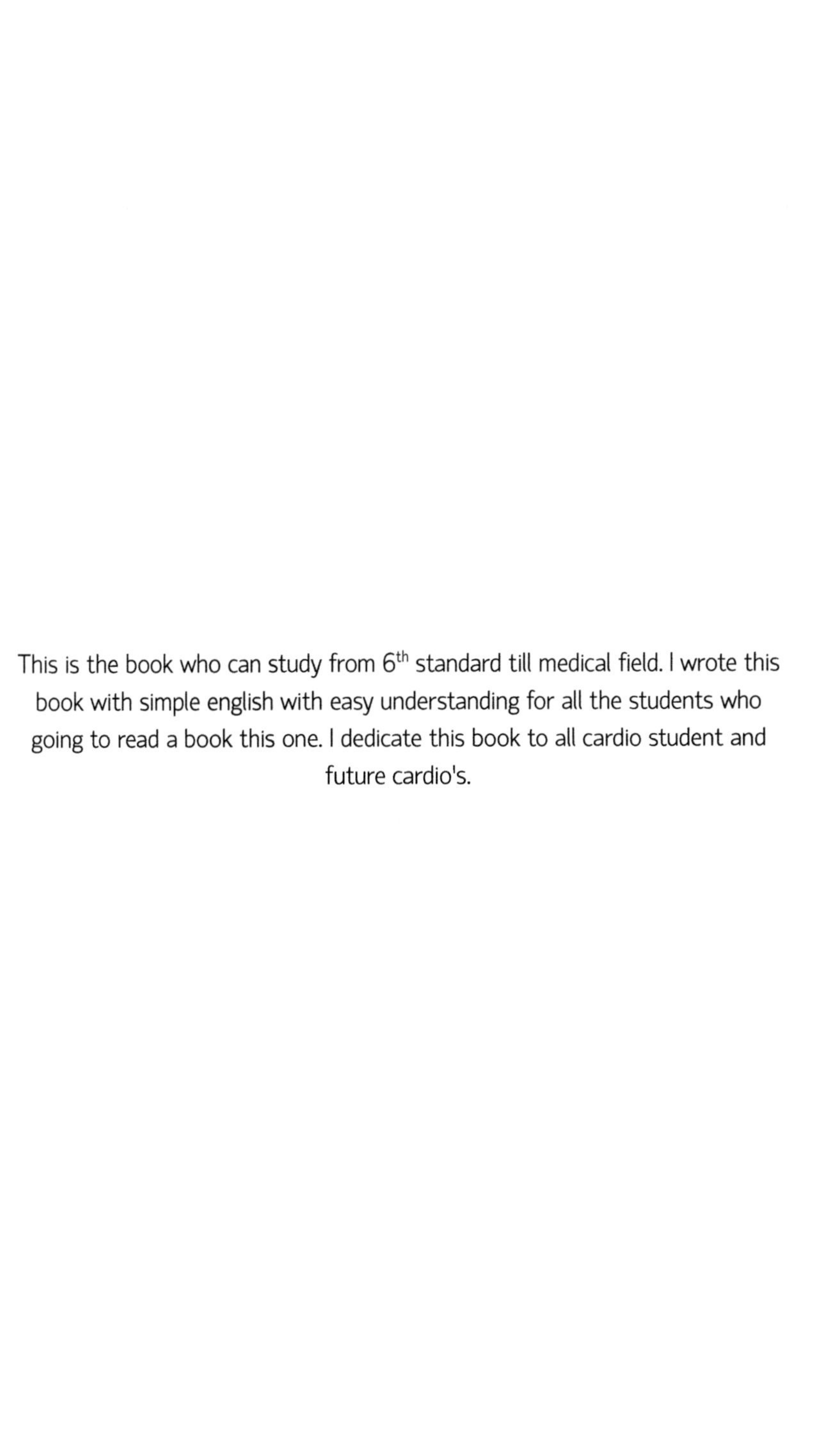

This is the book who can study from 6th standard till medical field. I wrote this book with simple english with easy understanding for all the students who going to read a book this one. I dedicate this book to all cardio student and future cardio's.

Contents

Foreword

It were well could one of the " men i have painted" take up the pen and contribute a character sketch of the " man who has painted me" for among all these living and admirable studies, it is doubtful if there is one indivdually more unusual or more interesting than that of the writer himself. to me, the lucky chance(if anything in this world is chance) that bought John McLure Hamilton to my Hawarden home in the early nineties was invaluable, for it was the beginning of a deeply valued friendship, of an intercourse rich in experience. Had i the pen of a De , Morgan let alone the tongue of men and angels, a book might have been written of the five.

Preface

Most of the adventures recorded in this book really occured; one or two were experience of my own, the rest those of boys who were schoolmates of mine.Huck Finn is drawn from life: Tom sawyer also, but not from an individual- be is a combination of the characteristics of three boys whom i knew, and therefore belongs to the composite order of archietecure.

- sujitha suresh

Acknowledgements

Special thanks to the people who worked so hard in the preparation of this book; My MOM-S.Ushasree, My DAD- M.Suresh , My BROTHER- S.Ganesh vicky, MY COLLEGE STAFFS, AND MY FRIENDS.Thanks for supporting me to publish book. They need credit for telling me when an idea was half-baked or i neede to be quiet and let someone else talk. Acknowledgement would be incomplete without thanking the people i worked with wile correcting too many problems on too many projects.

Prologue

'' we should start back'' gared urge as the woods began to grow dark around them.

'' the wilding are dead."

'' do the dead frieghten you"? gared did not rise to the bait. he was an old man, past fifty, and he had seen the lordlings come and go. " dead is dead" he said '' we have no business with the dead."

CHAPTER ONE

HUMAN HEART

The heart is a muscular organ in most animals that pumps blood through the blood vessels of the circulatory system. the pumped blood carries OXYGEN and NUTRIENTS to the body, while carrying metabolic waste such as carbon di oxide to the lungs. The humans the heart is approximately the size of a closed fist and is located in the between the lungs, in the middle compartment of the chest. In humans, other mammls and birds, the heart is divided into four chambers; upper left and right atria and lower left and right heart and their left counterparts as the left heart. fish in contrast, have two chambers an atrium and a ventricle, while reptiles have three chambers. in a healthy heart blood flows one way through the heart due to heart valves, which prevent backflow. The wall of the heart due to heart valves, which prevent backflow. The wall of the heart is made up of three layers; EPICARDIUM, MYOCARDIUM & ENDOCARDIUM. The heart pumps blood with a rhythm determined by a group of pacemaker cells in a sinoatrial node. the heart recieves blood flow in oxygen from the systemic circulation, through the lungs where it recieves oxygen and gives off carbondi oxide. Oxygenated blood returns to the left atrium, passes through the left ventricle and is pumped out through the aorta to the systemic circulation- where the oxygen is used and metabolized to carbon dioxide. The heart beats at a resting rate close to 72 beats per minute .Exercise temporarily increase the rate, but lowers resting heart fate in the long term, and is good for heart health.

STRUCTURE OF HUMAN HEART:

The human heart is situated in the mediastinum, at the level of the thoracic vertebrae T5-T8. A DOUBLE MEMBRANED SAC CALLED THRICARDIUM SURROUNDS THE HEART AND ATTACHES TO THE MEDIASTINUM. The back surface of the heart is the attachment point for several large blood vessels the venae cavae, aorta and pulmonary trunk. The upper part of the heart is located at the level of the third coastal cartilage. the lower tip of the heart, lies to the left of the sternum between junction of the fourth and fifth ribs nera their articulation with the coastal cartilages. the largest part of the heart is usually slightly offset to the leftside of the chest and is felt to be on the left because the left heart is stronger and larger since it pumps to all body parts. because the heart is between the lungs the the left lung is smaller than the right lung and has cardiac notch in its border to accomodate the heart. An adult heart has a mass of 250 gms- 350gms. The hear is often decribed as the size of a fist: 12cm in length, 8cm in wide, and 6cm in thickness, although this descripition is disputed as the heart is likely to be slightly larger. Well trained athletes can have much larger hearts due to the effects of exercise on the heart muscle, similar to the response of skeletal muscle.

DEVELOPMENT OF HUMAN HEART:

The heart is the first functional organ to develop and starts to beat and pump blood at about three weeks into embryogensis. this early start is crucial for subsequent and prenatal development.The heart derives from splanchnopleuric mesenchyme in the neural plate which forms the cardiogenic region.Two endocardial tubes from here that fuse to form a primitive heart tube known as the tubular heart between the third and fourth week, the heart tube lengthens and begins to fold to form an S shape within the pericardium. This places the chambers and major vessels into the correct alignment for the developed heart. Further development will include the formation of the septa and the valves and the remodelling of the heart chambers. By the end of the fifth week, the septa are complete and by the ninth week, the heart valves are complete. before the fifth week there is an opening in the fetal heart is known as FORAMEN OVALE. the foramen ovale allowed blood in the fetal heart to pass directly from the right atrium to the left atrium, allowing some blood to bypass the lungs. with the seconds after birth, a flap of tissue known as the SEPTUM PRIMUM that previously acted as a valve closes the foramen ovale was called the fossa ovalis. the embryonic heart begins beating around 22 days after conception. The embryonic heart rate then accelerates and reaches a peak rate of 165-185 bpm early in the early 7th week.After 9 weeks it starts to decelerate, slowing to around 145bpm at birth. There is no difference in female and male heart rates before birth.

CHAPTER TWO

HEART CHAMBER

- Hollow cavities within the heart for containing blood.
- Two smaller chambers called atrium are near the base, and two larger chambers called ventricle are close to the apex.
- RIGHT ATRIUM after recieving deoxygenated blood from body tissues through the superior and inferior vena cava, pumps the blood into the RIGHT VENTRICLE (RV) via the right atria ventricular orifice.RV then pumps the blood to the lungs for gas exchange, through the pulmonary trunk and arteries.
- LEFT ATRIUM after recieving oxygenated blood from the lungs through the pulmonary veins, pumps the blood into the left ventricle via the left atria ventricular orifice.
- LV then pumps the blood to the blood to the body tissues for supplying oxygen to every body cell, through the aorta.
- RA na LA are seprated by a central heart heart wall called interatrial septum, while RV and LV are separated by a interventricular septum.
- LV has a thicker myocardium layer and contains rough ridges called TRABECULAE CARNEAE. HEART ATTACK:
- A Heart attack occurs when the flow of blood to the heart is blocked. The blockage is most often buildup of fat, cholestro and other substances, which form a plaque in the atries that feed the heart CORONARY ARTEIRES .Sometimes, aplaque can rupture and form a clot that blocks blood flow. The interrupted blood flow can damage or destroy part of the heart muscle.A Heart attack, also called a ayocardial infraction, can be fatal, but treatment has improved dramatically over the years. Its crucial

to call 911 or emergency medical help if you think you might be having a heart attack.

SYMPTOMS:
Commen heart attacks signs and symptoms include:

- Pressure, tightness, pain, or a squeezing or aching sensation in your chest or arms that may spread to your neck, jaw or back
- Nausea, indigestion, heartburn or abdominal pain
- shortness of breath
- cold sweat
- fatigue
- lightheadedness or sudden dizziness.

CHAPTER THREE

HEART VALVES:

- Two heart valves located between atria and ventricles are called atrioventricular valves which include the tricuspid valve between RA and RV, and bicuspid valve between LA and LV.
- Two heart valves located at the existing arteries are called semilunar valves which include the plumonic semilunar valve at the base of pulmonary trunk, and the aortic semilunar valve at the base of aorta.
- Each AV valve consists of cusps(EXTENSION OF ENDOCARDIUM) Chordae tendineae, papillary muscles(the latter two are designed to prevent eversion of the cusps into the atria)
- AV valves prevent backflow into atria, while SL valves prevent backflow into ventricles. CIRCULATION PATHWAYS:
- PULMONARY CIRCUIT
- COONARY CIRCUIT PULMONARY CIRCUIT:
- Pulmonary circuit alows deoxygenated blood to be transported into the lungs for gas exchange, so that oxygenated blood can once again flows into the left heart.
- Deoxygenated blood from body tissue - superior & inferior vena cava - RA - tricuspid valve - RV - pulmonic SL valve - pulmonary arteries - lungs - oxygenated blood travels in pilmonary veins-LA - bicuspid valve - LV. CORONARY CIRCUIT
- Coronary circuit allows oxygenated blood to be delivered to cardiac muscle cells in the heart wall, and ots deoxygenated blood is drained back to the RA-

- Oxygenated blood in LV - aortic SL valve - aorta - arteries - arterioles - cappilaries in tissue -deoxygnated blood travels in venules - veins - superior & inferior vena cava - RA.
- Cardiac cycles are aminly controlled by nerve impulse, while hormones only can influence the heart rate.
- Two mechanisms to regulate cardiac cycles- intrinsic control and extrinsic control.
- INTRINSIC CONTROL consists of pacemakers and a conduction system.
- EXTRINSIC CONTROL consists of sympathetic and parasymapathetic nerves, and hormones, that influence the pace makera and affect the heart rate.

CHAPTER FOUR

ELECTROCARDIOGRAM;

- A graphic record of the electrical activity of the heart.
- P-WAVE - small upward wave representing atria depolarization - atrial systole occurs by the end of P wave so, the P wave is atrial excitation.
- P-Q INTERVAL : represents the conduction through the atria musculature, and AV delay.
- Q - WAVE: Action potentials spreads through the muscle of the septum between the ventricles, mostly from left to right and produce the samll, variable and usually negative wave, the Q wave.
- R-WAVE: Action potentials spreads through the big mass of ventricular muscle at the apex producing a large positive deflection, called the R- WAVE.
- S-WAVE: Action potential continues to spread through the last part of the bases of the ventricles, producing the usually inverted S wave.
- QRS - COMPLEX: indicates ventricular depolarization and coincides with atrial repolarization.
- S-T SEGMENT: indicate the time between ventricular depolarization and begining of repolarizarion.
- Q-T-INTERVAL: shows events in ventricular activity from begining of depolarization until end of repolarization.
- T-WAVE: Indicates the ventricular repolarization.

CHAPTER FIVE

CARDIODYNAMICS;

- A cardiac cycle consists of 3 phases of events.
- RELAXATION PERIOD: when all 4 heart chambers are relaxed, all 4 heart valves are closed, and blood is coming into the 2 atria through the veins.
- VENTRICULAR FILLING: When 70% of the blood in the atria flow passively into venticles due to gravity, followed by 30% of the blood being pumped by atrial systol during the phase, AV valves are open while SL valves are still closed.
- VENTRICULAR SYSTOLE: After all the blood in atria gets into ventricles, AV valves close, atria go into relaxation and ventricles contract to the pump the blood into exiting arties which opens the SL valves.
- SL VALVES will close after almost all ventriculkar blood is ejected there is always 60ml blood remained in each ventricle, a volume called END SYSTOLIC VOLUME or ESV. Then the ventricles relax and a new cardiac cycle will flow.
- Each cardiac cycle takes about 0.8 sec to complete.
- Toward the end of ventricullar filling, when pressure builds up in the ventricles AV valves begin to close.Now papillary muscles contract, pulling the chordae and cusps, to prevents eversion of the cusps into the atria.
- In each cardiac cycle, the two atria contract and relax simultaneously - a phenomenon called ATRIAL SYNCYTUM.The same is true for the ventricles, which is known as VENTRICULAR SYNCTUM.

CHAPTER SIX

CARDIAC CYCLE;

CARDIAC OUTPUT: Volume of blood pumped by the heart each minute = stroke volume (volume of each beat) x Heart rate (betas/ mins)

- STROKE VOLUME : Determined by the volume of blood in the heart at the beginning of systole minus the amount of blood remaining in the ventricles when the valves close at the end of systole.
- SV (ml/beat) = EDV(120 ml) - ESV (50 ml) =70 ml/beat.
- End diastolic volume is the amiount of blood that collects in a ventricle during diastole.
- End systolic volume is the amount of blood remainning in the ventricle after it has contracted.
- End systolic volume is the amiunt of blood remainning in the ventricle after it has contracted.

DEGREE OF STRETCH OF HEART MUSCLE:

Frank - starling law : stretching muscle fibres, increase their length and produces increased contractile force of the heart. The contractile force is the preload.

AUSCULATION:

- The process of studying heart sounds using a stethoscope.
- Each cardiac cycle generates 4 heart sounds, usually only the first two sounds are audible.
- S1 is the loudest, caused by the closure of AV VALVES at the beginning of ventricular diastole; it matches the T wave in ECG.

- S2 sound is second loudest caused by the closure of SL VALVES at beginning of ventricular diastole: it matches the T wave in ECG.
- S3 sound is noises generated by ventricular filling in the first 1/ 3 a trial blood being pumped into ventricules.
-

CHAPTER SEVEN

BLOOD PRESSURE:

- Blood pressure (120/80mm Hg)
- Systolic pressure is the highest pressure attained in the aorta and peripheral arteries when blood is ejected by the ventricles into the aorta.
- Diastolic pressure is the lowest pressure attained during relaxation or diastolic phase of the heat.
- Mean arterial blood pressure is the highest in the aorta and large arteries (100 Hg)..
- It sharply decreases in small arteries and even more in arterioles(30mmHg).
- After passage through the cappilaries and in the small veins the pressure is about 15 mmHg.
- It falls to about 5mm Hg upon entering the R.atrium. RISK FACTORES FOR STROKE:
- ALCHOL CONSUMPTION
- DIABETES
- ELEVATED SERUM CHOLESTROL
- FAMILY HISTORY OF CARDIOVASCULAR DISEASE
- HYPERTENSION
- SMOKING
- TRANSIENT ISCEMIC ATTACKS ATHEROSCLEROSES:
- Atherosclerosis of atries can occlude blood flow to the heart and brain and is a causative factor it up to 505 of all deaths in U.S.A., EUROPE., and JAPAN.
- Atherosclerosis begins with injury to endothelium, the movement of monocytes and lymphocytes into the tunica

interna and the conversion of monocytes into the macrophages that engulf the lipids.

- Atherosclerosis is promoted by such risk factors as smoking, hypertension, and high plasma cholestrol concentration.
- LDLs which carry cholestrol into the artery wall, are oxidized by the endothelium and are a major contibutor to atherosclerosis.
- Occlusion of blood flow in the coronary arteries by atherosclerosis may produce ischemia of the heart muscle and angina pectoris, which may lead to myocardial infraction.
- The EKG can be used to detect abnormal cardiac rates, abnormalconduction between the atria and ventricles, and other abnormal patterns of electrial conduction in the heart.

THANK YOU

9 798886 843248

Printed by Libri Plureos GmbH in Hamburg,
Germany